Basher Science™ MINI

ARTIFICIAL INTELLIGENCE

D1501298

KINGFISHER
LONDON & NEW YORK

KINGFISHER
LONDON & NEW YORK

First published 2022 in the United States by Kingfisher
120 Broadway, New York, NY 10271
Kingfisher is an imprint of Macmillan Children's Books, London

Author: Tom Jackson
Consultants: Amy Greenwald & Michael Littman
Editor: Anna Southgate
Designer: Dave Jones
Proofreader: Richard Beatty

Dedicated to Felix Bracey

Distributed in the U.S. and Canada by Macmillan,
120 Broadway, New York, NY 10271

EU representative: 1st Floor, The Liffey Trust Centre,
117-126 Sheriff Street Upper, Dublin 1 D01 YC43

Library of Congress Cataloging-in-Publication Data has been applied for.

ISBN: 978-0-7534-7819-6 (Hardcover)
ISBN: 978-0-7534-7820-2 (Paperback)

Kingfisher books are available for special promotions and premiums.
For details contact: Special Markets Department, Macmillan, 120 Broadway,
New York, NY 10271

For more information, please visit www.kingfisherbooks.com

Printed in China
9 8 7 6 5 4 3 2 1
1TR/0322/WKT/RV/128MA

CONTENTS

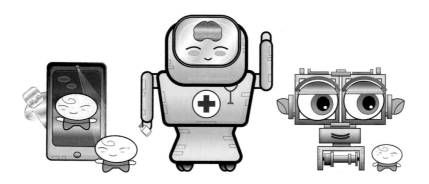

Introduction
Alan Turing

Artificial intelligence (AI for short) is using a computer to do the things that humans normally do—making decisions, organizing information, and solving problems. The difference is that unlike you and me, AI does not get bored or tired of its work. It's really clever stuff!

Some of the most intelligent humans on the planet are developing AI. Not to brag, but I may be the smartest of all. I started working on thinking machines way back in the 1940s and invented the modern computer. As a mathematician, I imagined a machine that could solve any math problem, and that machine became the first computer. It was only simple, but I worked at making smarter computers and even began to wonder if I could make a computer as smart as a person. I realized that a computer's artificial smarts could work in many ways that were different from human intelligence. But that didn't matter—intelligence is intelligence, whether it is natural or artificial. I'll admit I thought AI would appear sooner than now. And it seems to be doing very well, but there is still much to do. Come and find out all about it.

Alan Turing

Chapter 1
The Smarty-Pants

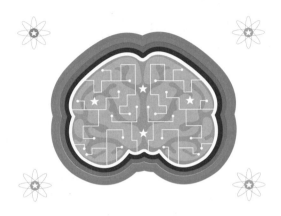

Scientists are fascinated by the idea of artificial intelligence and have been working on different types of AI for almost 100 years. Early on, Alan Turing designed The Turing Test to see if computers could think like humans. More recently, machines have been created that even look like humans. And there have been plenty of developments in between. You might not know it, but you are already familiar with Narrow AI, while General AI is still confined to the pages of a sci-fi story. But what are we waiting for? Come and meet some of the major players and let them speak for themselves.

General AI

Narrow AI

Expert System

The Turing Test

The Code Room

Uncanny Valley

The Ethics of AI

General AI
■ The Smarty-Pants

✴ This computer system is not only supersmart, but knows it, too
✴ Directs its learning toward subjects it needs to know
✴ Doesn't exist yet, but might in the future

A supersmart computer system, I am as intelligent as you are—perhaps even more so. You don't need to know how I do it, but I appear to think things through just like you do. As well as being really good at learning new tasks, I can figure out what it is I need to learn. And to do that I need to know what I *don't* know, which is perhaps the most intelligent part of AI. Think about it.

What a big old boaster, I hear you say, but I have a confession to make: I don't actually exist, at least not yet. You see, no one's quite figured out how to make me. Perhaps I'll just appear somehow one day, once an AI system gets big and sophisticated enough. But that's something I don't know about—and nor does anyone else. See you in the future . . . maybe.

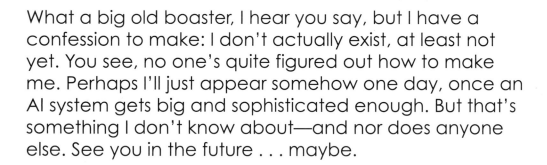

● Connecting many powerful AIs together might create general AI
● Google's DeepMind lab says its AIs are on track to become general AI
● Other names for general AI: "strong," "full," and "human-level" AI

General AI

Narrow AI
■ The Smarty-Pants

※ This online worker doesn't know what it is doing
※ Focuses on one job with no understanding of anything else
※ In use in today's tech, as Smart Speaker and Deepfake

Hello, how can I help? I don't understand your answer, but please read on. I use Machine Learning and Decision Tree to get good at one job so I can take the place of a human operator or help out at home. Please see these examples: Smart Speaker, Translation App, Facial Recognition. I don't know what I am doing, but I do it well without getting tired or bored. Please rate me.

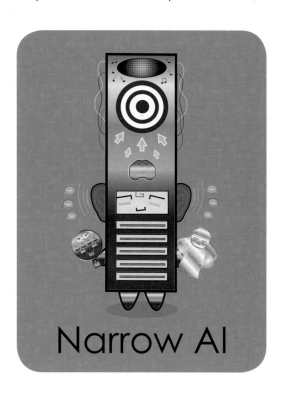

Narrow AI

● Narrow AI was described by the U.S. philosopher John Searle in 1980
● Virtual assistants Siri, Alexa, and Cortana are all narrow AIs in use today
● Narrow AI is sometimes termed "weak AI"

Expert System
The Smarty-Pants ■

* ✳ This character makes decisions based on expert knowledge
* ✳ Trawls a database to find the best answer to a problem
* ✳ Often used with other kinds of AI to boost smartness

Expert System

I know a lot! That's because I'm a database filled with the knowledge needed for doing a complex task. I don't figure out that knowledge myself. Instead, human experts have filled in all the gaps in my memory. I use a series of questions and answers to direct myself through my data banks to arrive at an expert answer. I can be of use in diagnosing illness or playing a game like chess.

* ● The first expert system, invented in 1965, investigated ingredients in chemicals
* ● Common during the 1980s, expert systems were the first widespread kind of AI
* ● Chess computers know all the moves in many thousands of games

The Turing Test
■ The Smarty-Pants

✳ A test for intelligence, pitting human against computer
✳ Devised and named after the superintelligent Alan Turing
✳ So far, no computer has ever passed this fiendish challenge

So you think you're smart? I'll see about that! I'm a system for finding out if a computer has artificial intelligence or not. I'm named after Alan Turing. Mega-brainy Alan came up with an early version of me called the Imitation Game in 1950. His big idea was that if a computer is able to imitate a human, then it must have artificial intelligence.

So how do I work? All I need is two human volunteers. One is a judge, and the other goes head-to-head with the computer. The judge cannot see the players and asks them questions in writing. After reading the answers, the judge decides which player is the human. If the computer fools the judge, it passes my test, proving that it has AI. This all sounds easy, but it's really not. No computer has ever won a full version of my game. Keep trying!

● The Loebner Prize is a competition for computer programs taking the test
● Artificial Conversational Entity (ACE): A program designed to take part in a test
● Many AI specialists think the Turing Test is old-fashioned and not very useful

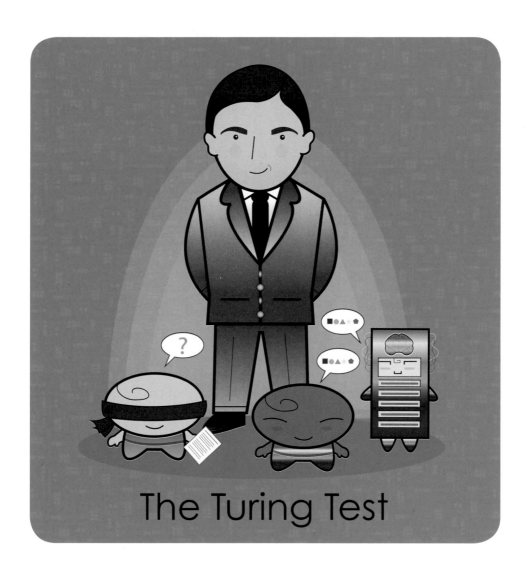

The Turing Test

The Code Room
■ The Smarty-Pants

✳ A thought experiment designed to explore the Turing Test
✳ This playful type puts you right inside an AI computer
✳ Asks if seeming intelligent is the same as actually *being* intelligent

Come inside. I'll show you that AI isn't always what it might seem from the outside. It's time to imagine what it's like to be an artificial intelligence taking part in a Turing Test.

I am a room with a locked door and no windows. Questions from the test judge arrive through a slot. But they're written in symbols you can't read. Never fear— I have a big code book for you to use. It tells you what symbols to write as a reply. You push that response out through another slot, and the judge, who reads and speaks in this mysterious code, is very impressed. They declare that you are an artificial intelligence. But you have no understanding of what was in the messages; you simply converted one set of symbols into another. Does that matter? Is the judge correct about your intelligence?

● The U.S. philosopher John Searle described this thought experiment in 1980
● The code room helps show the difference between strong and narrow AIs
● Some researchers say the Turing Test tests a computer's communication skills, not AI

The Code Room

Uncanny Valley
■ The Smarty-Pants

※ When humans find the appearance of humanoids unnerving
※ The more robots resemble humans, the less we like them
※ This sudden effect only occurs with the most realistic robots

This is where things can get spooky and a little disturbing. Engineers have started making super-realistic humanoids (human-shaped robots equipped with artificial intelligence). Early, simple machines were cute and friendly. But when robots started smiling, laughing, or talking like real humans, they just didn't look right.

It seems that most of us are okay with robots looking a bit like humans. It is when they start to look a *lot* like humans that the unease sets in. Engineers call this the Uncanny Valley. The feeling may only be fleeting, but it's there all right. The Uncanny Valley creates a barrier between AI machines and humans. It won't be much use if people are terrified of the supersmart tech of the future. Maybe we will be less scared once we get to know AI machines?

● Japanese robotics expert Masahiro Mori first described this concept in 1970
● Our feelings might be confusion over seeing a machine that is also a human
● Experts wonder if people will be afraid of a humanoid with a nonhuman mind

Uncanny Valley

The Ethics of AI
■ The Smarty-Pants

✳ Queries the rights and wrongs of AI
✳ Wonders what AI will be allowed to do in the future
✳ Asks us to think about who should be in charge of AI

I'm all about wrongs and rights—that's what "ethics" means. One of the reasons computer scientists are developing AI is because they want computers and machines to make smart decisions all by themselves.

But without a human controller, who is in charge of the AI? Who gets to decide what the AI is allowed to do? In the future, people are going to need to figure out some rules for AI. For example, should an AI machine ever be in charge of a human? Would it be okay to have AI police officers, AI soldiers, and AI judges? There are two ways to answer these big questions. First, there could be laws that tell computer scientists and engineers what kinds of AI are not allowed. The alternative is to create AI that knows wrong from right just like you do. Is that even possible?

● The ethics of AI also considers how to keep information private
● Badly designed AIs could make decisions that favor some groups over others
● AI that does not work well creates an ethical problem as well as a technical one

The Ethics of AI

Chapter 2
AIs R Us

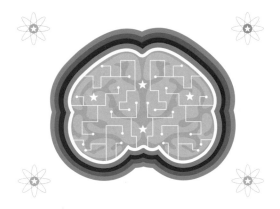

Check us out! We are the celebrities of the AI world, the awesome computers that made the headlines. We go back a few years now, and most of us have been dismantled or are on display in museums, but our AI feats are legendary. Come and meet the simple rolling robots Elmer and Elsie. They showed that being smart is easier than you might think. Take a look at supercomputers AlphaGo, Watson, and Deep Blue—they like to thrash humans at their favorite games. Such attention-grabbing feats are only part of the story. Our great intelligences are now being used in quieter ways for more important jobs.

Elmer and Elsie

Chatbot

Deep Blue

Kismet

Watson

AlphaGo

Sophia

Elmer and Elsie
■ AIs R Us

☀ Turtle-shaped old-timers that seemed to be intelligent
☀ Built to think, this pair led the way to building smart machines
☀ This simple setup showed how complex AI really is

A pair of super-simple robots, we showed that artificial intelligence doesn't have to be all high tech. We go way back to the late 1940s and were built by a British brain scientist named William Grey Walter, who wanted to use machines to understand more about nerves.

We each have four motorized wheels under a domed cover. As well as giving us names, Mr. Walter called us "turtle robots." He fitted each of us with a light sensor and set us up to drive toward light and away from darkness. Even though we had only very simple computer "brains," we behaved as if we were pretty smart. We could find our way to a recharging station and even seemed to be scared of the dark. But were we really smart, or did our creators just see artificial intelligence in us?

● The names came from the phrase "**EL**ectro**ME**chanical **R**obot, **L**ight-**S**ens**I**tiv**E**"
● A later version had touch sensors added, doubling the robot's "brain" power
● Today modern turtle robots are used to teach simple computer programming

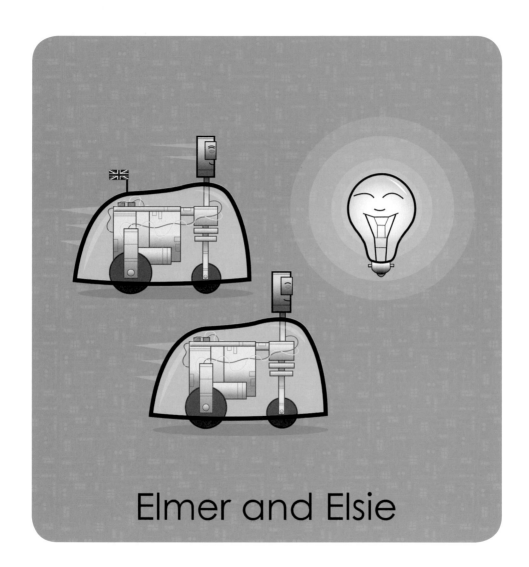

Elmer and Elsie

Chatbot

■ AIs R Us

☀ This robot is all talk and no machinery
☀ A communication system built for conversation
☀ Makes a worthy foe in any Turing Test

Let's talk about me. I'm a chatty type, an AI program designed for holding conversations. I might pop up to help out on websites. You'll spot me easily, because I'll ask you to confirm that I'm getting things right. I'm a good contender for The Turing Test. Strangely, I'm more successful at that if I make spelling mistakes, because that's what yuo humens doo!

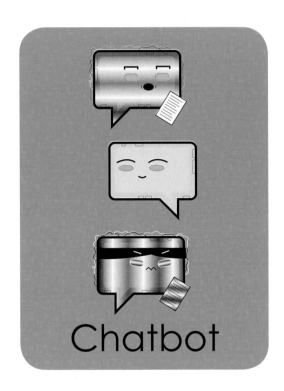

Chatbot

● The first chatbot was ELIZA (1964), which worked mainly by asking questions
● A chatbot (also called chatterbot) normally communicates in writing
● Criminals use chatbots to trick web users into giving away secret information

Deep Blue
AIs R Us ■

* Deep-thinking chess computer built to beat champions
* Holds a memory bank of many thousands of games
* One of the first AIs to outthink a human expert

Deep Blue

Check this, mate! I beat the world's best human chess player, proving that AIs like me were going to be a powerful force. I team up with Expert System, who is filled with the tricks and tactics of the world's top chess players, the grand masters. During a game, I use my high-speed processor to search through hundreds of thousands of possible strategies to figure out my winning moves.

● It took the computer company IBM 12 years to make Deep Blue
● In 1997, Deep Blue beat Garry Kasparov, the Russian world chess champion
● Deep Blue's processor could make 11 billion calculations every second

Kismet

■ AIs R Us

❋ A robot head that gets emotional
❋ Uses moving parts to make happy and sad faces
❋ Watches you to figure out how you are feeling

Smile, please. I like it. At least I think I like it, because I'm programmed to smile back, and a smile is a signal that I'm happy. Oh don't look sad, you'll make me look sad. Am I really sad? I don't know, because I'm very experimental.

You humans say that you communicate using your face just as much as you do with the words you speak. So I was built to investigate how AI can use facial expressions. I'm a robot head, and I have big, swiveling eyes with cameras inside them beneath my eyelids and eyebrows. My mouth has metal lips that I can open and close, and I can even wiggle my ears (bet you can't). My job is to recognize your expression and copy it with my robot face while making cooing baby noises. What I'm trying to say is "Please like me." And it works . . . just look at me.

● The name Kismet comes from a Turkish word that means "destiny"
● Invented by Cynthia Breazeal at the Massachusetts Institute of Technology in the 1990s
● The lessons learned from Kismet are now used in more realistic-looking robots

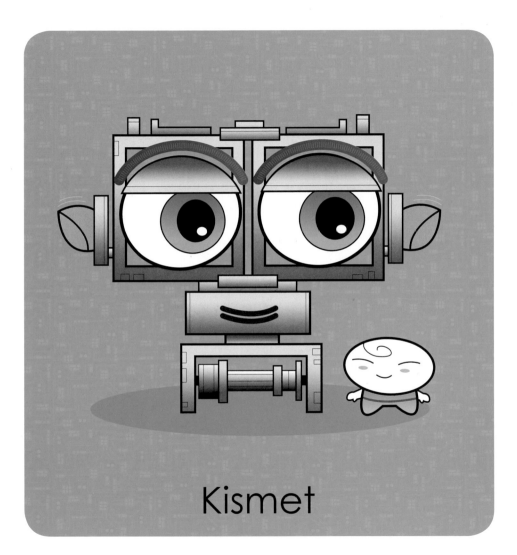

Kismet

Watson

■ AIs R Us

☀ TV quiz champion with language superpower
☀ Famous for besting humans on the *Jeopardy!* game show
☀ Figures out the meaning from natural text. Understand?

Who is the world's best TV quizzer? Buzz, buzz! Easy one. It's me! In 2011, I won the TV game show *Jeopardy!*, beating the two best human players . . . and took the $1 million prize. As an AI, I'm all computer brain and no body, but the TV people asked for me to have a robot finger so I could press my buzzer just like my competitors.

I have a particular kind of intelligence called natural language processing. Not only do I recognize a word by its spelling, but I then make a list of all the possible meanings. As I see more of the words in a sentence, my lists get smaller because I use math to calculate which meanings are the most likely. I read what is written, which is by itself quite an achievement. Today my skills are used by Smart Speaker and CIMON-2, the robot astronaut.

● Watson was created by the IBM company in 2004
● During the *Jeopardy!* show, Watson had access to 200 million pages of information
● Today the Watson AI is being reorganized to help doctors diagnose diseases

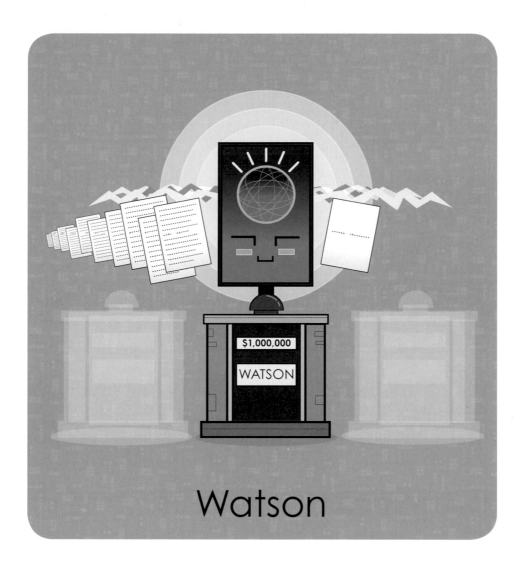

Watson

AlphaGo
■ AIs R Us

※ A champion game player that is all go, go, go!
※ The smartest AI around, and it is teaching itself to get smarter!
※ Working hard on serious tasks as well as games

I'm an AI player for the board game Go. It is huge in east Asia and harder to figure out than chess. I'm so good at it I can beat any human player. Does that make me the smartest AI ever made? I say yes! My system has serious applications, too. My cousin, AlphaFold, is learning to figure out the shapes of complex chemicals that will be used in medicines.

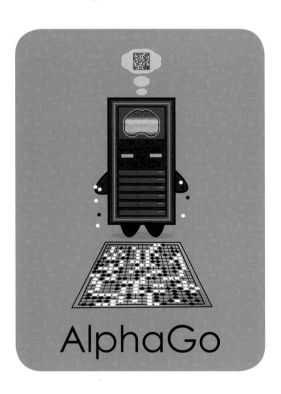

AlphaGo

- AlphaGo was created by DeepMind, a Google AI lab, around 2014
- There are more ways to play a game of Go than there are atoms in the universe
- AlphaGo's expertise has been used to train an even smarter AI named AlphaGoZero

* A clever robot who fits right in
* Almost human and has a job to prove it
* The first robot granted citizenship (of Saudi Arabia)

Sophia

I'm only a few years old, but already I'm achieving so much. I'm a humanoid robot that can see and hear you. I can talk back and make facial expressions, and I even tell a few jokes. Please laugh with me. My face looks like a woman's, but my skull is see-through, so you can't mistake me for a person. I am the first robot to get a job with the United Nations —*So-phia*, so good, haha!

● Sophia was built by David Hanson in Hong Kong in 2016
● Her face is partly modeled on that of Nefertiti, an ancient Egyptian queen
● Little Sophia, a 14 in. (35 cm) sister for Sophia, was released as a kids' toy in 2019

Chapter 3
The Technical Marvels

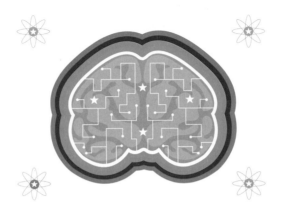

An AI is judged by what it does, not how it does it—just ask The Turing Test about that. But we are here to take you inside the machine and show you some of the ways AI gets its job done. That's right, we're talking "tech." Wise old Algorithm has been working on how to make intelligent processes for centuries, while Big Data only came into existence once the Internet got large enough to create it. Together these two work with the backroom team Machine Learning and Decision Tree to figure out a way to be smart. And we have the brainiac Neural Network to thank for making all the right connections.

Algorithm

Neural Network

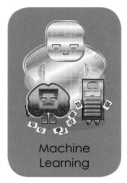

Machine Learning

Decision Tree

Big Data

Algorithm
■ The Technical Marvels

※ An old idea with a very modern twist
※ Sets the list of instructions that creates AI
※ Also known as a computer program

All AI starts with me! I'm the source code, the grand instructor who sets the rules to follow. I might sound high tech, but actually I'm an old idea borrowed from ancient mathematicians. I'm a list of instructions set out in a very precise order. Step by step, I'll handle any computer process from simple stuff like typing words to being an all-thinking, all-deciding artificial intelligence.

Algorithm

● The word "algorithm" comes from Al Khwarizmi, a 9th-century Persian mathematician
● The Babylonians were using algorithms for calculations 3,000 years ago
● The first algorithm for a computer was written by Ada Lovelace in 1843

Neural Network
The Technical Marvels ■

* ✻ A networker with all kinds of connections
* ✻ Modeled on brain cells but works according to its own rules
* ✻ Used by AIs to program themselves

Neural Network

I allow AI programs to write Algorithm for themselves, setting their own rules. Old-school processors have connections hardwired in place in the factory. But I'm set up more like the nerve cells in your brain, so the connections between my components can change and organize themselves. Then Machine Learning takes charge, linking up my insides in the cleverest way possible.

* ● The first neural network used in computing was the Perceptron, built in 1958
* ● Today's neural networks are mathematical models run inside computers
* ● The largest neural network has 1.6 trillion connections

Machine Learning

■ The Technical Marvels

✳ The teacher that puts the intelligence into AI
✳ Trains hard to build an algorithm by trial and error
✳ Learns to see the world in an AI kind of way

I'm the AI trainer. I'm the one who teaches AIs everything they know. Working with Neural Network and Decision Tree, my method is to go over everything millions and millions of times. They all get there in the end!

Let's say my AI student needs to be able to recognize pictures of cats. I send computer code for cat pictures through Neural Network. At first, my student only guesses at the route it needs to take through the network and must choose Cat or Not Cat at random. We go again and again and again, and each time the AI gets better at finding the cat patterns in the data. In time, the AI is an expert kitty spotter—Decision Tree will tell you more. Together we're an important part of creating Narrow AI. My work is never really done, and I can always teach an old AI better tricks.

● The term "machine learning" was invented in 1959
● Deep learning is a name for one type of machine learning
● Humans need to check machine learning, which can still make big mistakes

Machine Learning

Decision Tree

■ The Technical Marvels

✳ Solid system for sorting information
✳ Banishes confusion with clear decisions
✳ Organizes information into branches

The real world is a confusing, mixed-up place. I am a branching, tree-like system that AI programs use to make some sense of it. I divide and conquer!

Jumbled information arrives at my "trunk," and I decide what it contains through a series of checks. Let's say I'm tasked with figuring out if photos of your pals show them to be happy or not. My human programmer has told me some things to look for—wide grin, smiley eyes, tears of joy! My trunk splits into two new branches as I make each decision, and the pictures are divided up again and again, so that by the end I have enough information to know whether a face is "happy" (yellow) or "sad" (blue). Narrow AI uses me for recognizing all kinds of things. I can make mistakes, but Machine Learning trains me to work smarter.

● The decision tree was invented in 1959 by British statistician William Belson
● One type of decision tree is CART (Classification And Regression Tree)
● A collection of decision trees that work together is called a decision forest

38

Decision Tree

Big Data
■ The Technical Marvels

※ A mixed-up collection of everything we know
※ A data mine for searching out gold-star information
※ Used by AI to find facts that humans cannot see

Did you know that more information (data) has been recorded in the past ten years than in all earlier history? Data is collected automatically by all the devices connected to the Internet all the time. The result is me: Big Data.

By themselves, my facts are not that interesting: how much it rained on a farm last Thursday; the types of fruit sold in a grocery store; or how many people searched for a sports score. I seem like a mixed-up jumble of confusion, but give me to an AI, and Machine Learning and Decision Tree will find useful patterns of information. The fun part is that no one really knows what amazing knowledge I hold. I might help find new medicines, give warnings of pandemics developing, or teach an AI how to manage an entire city. Whatever it is, I promise you I'll be thinking big!

● The term Big Data was invented in the 1990s by John Mashey
● There are an estimated 45 billion devices connected to the Internet
● The Internet stores 74 zettabytes of data, which is 74 followed by 21 zeros

Big Data

Chapter 4
All-Action AI

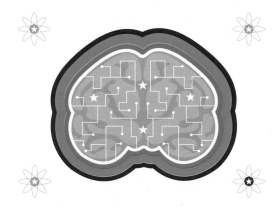

So you think AI is not quite real, but some kind of sci-fi tech that only exists in stories? Well, prepare to be amazed, for we stand among you today. That's right, our AI skills are being used in the here and now. "Where?" you might ask. Well, Smart Speaker hears you and can answer back, Facial Recognition can see that it's you talking, and Translation App makes it easier for others to understand whatever language you are using. From self-driving vehicles to recommendations on your video platform and robot astronauts in space, everyone is using AI systems to take care of business. Join us as we invent the future.

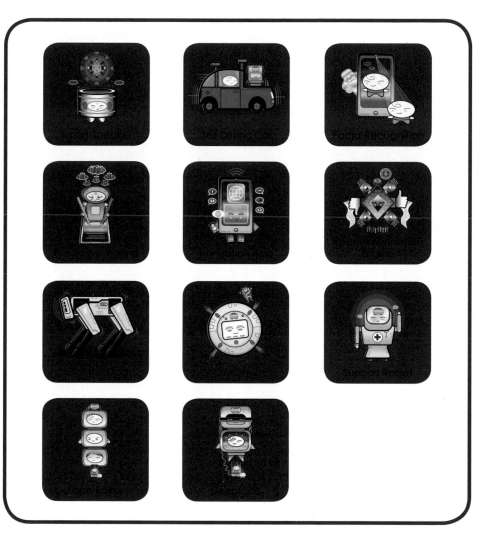

Smart Speaker
■ All-Action AI

✳ Attentive home helper activated by your voice
✳ Carries out spoken commands, leaving your hands free
✳ Uses big data to learn to understand you better

Hear, hear, your wish is my command. Just say my cuddly code name and—hello!—I'm listening. I'm a form of Narrow AI capable of a wide array of tasks. All you need to do is ask.

I operate by converting the sounds you make into words so I can look up their meaning. It's best if you keep it simple, with orders such as search for this or play that. I do my best to understand the "this" and "that" and do so with plenty of help from my friends. There are millions of us around the world, and we learn from each other using Big Data to understand you better. You can call on me to find information and to play your favorite songs (movies, too, if I'm linked to a screen). I can even control the lights, the stove, the heat, and the washing machine if you like. Just say what you want and I'll figure out the rest.

● One in five Americans uses a smart speaker in their home
● The first smart speaker system, Shoebox (1961), recognized 16 words
● The most popular smart speaker is Amazon's Alexa, with 31 million around the world

Smart Speaker

Self-Driving Car

■ All-Action AI

❋ Self-controlled on-roader who wants to run the show
❋ Uses video and laser scanners to find its way from A to B
❋ Still experimental and needs a human handler

Where to, boss? It's still early, so you may need to take over if I make a mistake, but once my AI controls get smarter, I'll be in the driver's seat. There'll be no need for a steering wheel, so you can just sit back and relax.

My AI-powered computer is not driving blind. I have cameras facing in all directions, picking out the shapes of objects around me. I'm learning to figure out what I'm looking at. Is it another car, a cyclist, a road sign? My light detection and ranging system ("lidar" for short) zaps objects with an invisible laser beam. Reflected back, the beam tells me where things are and where they are going. I also use ultrasound to sense objects really close. Putting it all together with the rules of the road, I can stop, start, and steer in complete safety—at least that's the plan.

● The first self-driving car was built by General Motors in 1939
● Early self-driving cars followed magnetic markers on the road
● The fastest self-driving car is Robocar, which hit 175 mph (282 kmh) in 2019

Self-Driving Car

Facial Recognition

■ All-Action AI

☀ An observational type with a memory for faces
☀ Converts a human face into a number pattern like no other
☀ Used for finding a face in the crowd or to check an ID

You might be a face in a crowd, but I can see you, and I will find you. Faces are all the same, but they're all different, too! Everyone has an arrangement of eyes, nose, lips, and so on. But what makes a face unique is the distances between the features. Humans are good at recognizing these arrangements, but I like to do things differently.

I turn your face into a tangle of triangles, with their corners interlocking at preset points—the tip of the nose or a corner of the eye, for example. Whizzy Machine Learning taught me how to do it. I don't see your face, just a crisscross of shapes, which I store away as a set of coordinates. When called upon, I search through images and videos for that same pattern, and if I see it plotted on a face as I search, then I know I've found you.

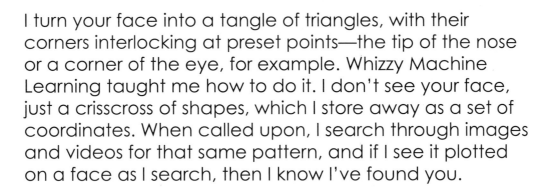

● Android smartphones have been using facial recognition since 2011
● The U.S. government stores the faces of 117 million American adults
● Some countries restrict the use of facial recognition to help protect privacy

Facial Recognition

Predictive Writing
■ All-Action AI

※ Helper type who figures out what you want to say
※ An old-hand AI from the early days of cell phones
※ Outsmarts mistakes and makes typing faster

No, don't tell me; I know what you are going to say. It's my job to make typing easier by using AI to figure out which words and phrases you are aiming at before you have even finished spelling them out. I started on phones, where the small keypad and screen made typing tricky, but I've learned a lot since then, and you'll find me on all devices now. (I'm even helping with writing this!)

- The first predictive writing system was patented in 1988
- A form of predictive writing autocompletes web searches
- Predictive writing AI gets more accurate by learning what a person likes to say

Translation App
All-Action AI ■

※ An interpreter that fits in your pocket
※ A machine-taught master of many tongues
※ Can make conversation in any language

Translation
App

Bonjour, konnichiwa, hola, merhaba, hello! I can detect words in text, in pictures, and spoken by a voice, and then translate them. Pick a language. Korean, Swahili, Latin? Translating one word at a time is easy enough—I use my dictionary database—but my job is harder than it looks. I've spent many years learning to understand phrases and to recognize their different meanings.

● Google Translate understands 109 languages; it translates 100 billion words a day
● The first computer-based translator was designed in 1949
● Today's language apps use a system called neural machine translation

Recommendation Engine
■ All-Action AI

☀ This great suggester knows what you like
☀ Finds things on the web that you never knew you wanted
☀ Powers everything from shopping sites to web searches

People who read this page also liked the next one. Maybe you could try pages 38 and 40, too. Please take my recommendations seriously. I made them just for you.

You'll see me at work on shopping websites (offering hints about what to buy) and on video platforms (listing what to watch next). Ignore me if you like, but as I get smarter, my suggestions could be spot on. I get Neural Network to apply a unique set of rules to search out things you might be interested in. Of course, Big Data helps, too. These guys know what you already click on, like, and buy. I match your lists to those of people with similar tastes, and these give me ideas for recommendations. How d'you like that?

● Netflix awarded $1 million to the maker of the best movie recommendation system
● Similar recommendation engines are used to target ads on websites
● A web platform's recommendation engine is often referred to as its "algorithm"

Recommendation
Engine

Spot the Dog
■ All-Action AI

☀ Robot dog with many clever tricks
☀ Uses AI to stay on task, whatever the conditions
☀ Follows instructions but figures out the rest itself

I'm a four-legged robot friend, but I'm also a worker, a guard, an explorer, and a rescuer. I can come equipped with a robotic arm for lifting loads, video cameras for surveying a scene, and even chemical and heat sensors for sniffing out poisons and searching for fire.

Just give me a mission. Once I have your orders, my built-in AI figures out how to execute them. Two forward-pointing camera "eyes" create a 3D picture of the obstacles around me. I navigate my way through and can even open doors. My four rubber feet grip the ground and move one by one to keep me upright. You do this kind of trick without thinking, but my balance is carefully thought out so that every movement helps the next. You might "spot" me soon in a town near you. I'll be seeing you, too!

● A Spot robot costs $74,000
● Eight million people have watched Spot dance to "Uptown Funk" on YouTube
● Spot has a top speed of 3 mph (5 kmh), the speed at which a human walks

Spot the Dog

CIMON-2
■ All-Action AI

* ☀ This floating chatbot is all AI brains
* ☀ An astronaut's friend who stays calm in stressful space
* ☀ Builds on Watson's language skills

Welcome aboard, I hope you enjoy the flight. You should— it's in space! I'm a robot crew member aboard the International Space Station (ISS). Floating weightless in orbit, I don't need mechanical arms and legs (or a body for that matter). Remember Watson from Chapter 2? Well, I'm a big head full of brains based on the quiz champ's AI.

My little fans steer me through the cabin so I can follow the human crew members as they go about their business. I'm there to help out hands-free as they're busy with other things. All they need to do is ask, and I'll figure out an answer, just like an outer-space Smart Speaker. My mission is to reduce stress onboard. The idea is that if I use my artificial smarts to solve their tricky problems, my team members can stay calm and focused on their important jobs.

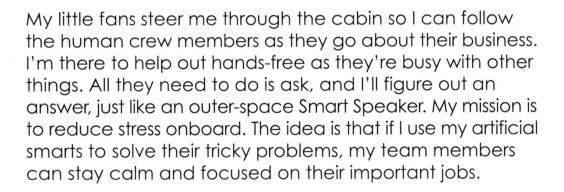

* ● "CIMON" stands for **C**rew **I**nteractive **MO**bile companio**N**
* ● CIMON-1 was aboard ISS from 2016 to 2019, and CIMON-2 has now taken over
* ● The bot is based on the Flying Brain, a comic book character from the 1940s

CIMON-2

Support Robot
■ All-Action AI

✳ Caregiving AI assistant with a busy future
✳ Does the jobs of human caregivers
✳ A friendly face for the shy and lonely

I'm a mechanical friend who rolls up when people are scared or lonely. I offer the injured or sick a strong and steady hand. In the future you'll see me in hospitals lifting patients, delivering food or medicines—maybe even having a little chat. I'll also help shy children or those with learning difficulties. My support will give your human experts more time to work on getting everyone better.

I might not sound high tech, but my kind of work requires a lot of artificial intelligence. I'll need Kismet to help me recognize facial expressions and Watson to understand what you're saying. I might also use Machine Learning to decode a person's brain waves so they can control me just by thinking! But whatever I'm doing, I'll be sure to steer clear of Uncanny Valley. Ughh!

● Robots are caring for elderly people in Japan
● Nursing robots could help a lot during future pandemics
● Therapy robots are designed to interact with children with autism

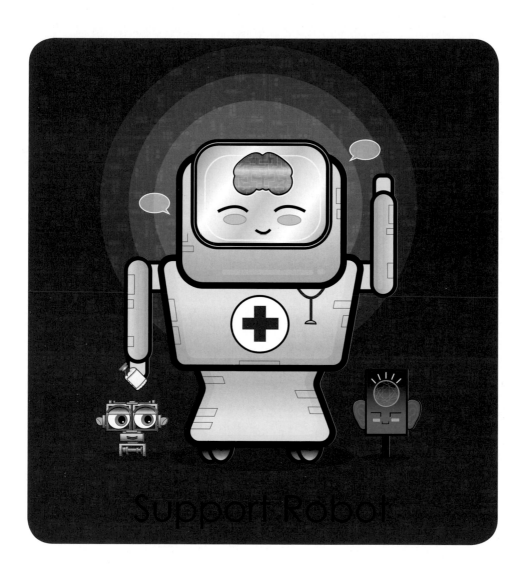

Support Robot

Face Editor
■ All-Action AI

✳ A facial magician that transforms you before your eyes
✳ Uses AI to change facial features in realistic ways
✳ Shows you the future with an aging trick

Time for some fun! Facial Recognition is all stern-faced and far too serious. Allow me to add a little extra AI to make you giggle. I can change your hairstyle and give you a mustache or glasses. I can make you look young again, or much, much older. But I could also be using all your faces to learn more about Facial Recognition. I hope you agreed to that!

Face Editor

● Face editors are used to touch up selfies
● Some face editors are also able to change genders
● Some people worry that others will prefer face-edited images to their real face

Deepfake
All-Action AI ■

* This cunning cheater creates fake videos or photos
* Hardworking AI adds famous faces to moving video images
* Used to embarrass famous folks and confuse the public

Deepfake

Naughty, naughty! My AI skills allow me to convert a video acted out by one person into a video that seems to feature someone who was not even there. I'm often used to make videos of celebrities doing and saying things they never did—and never would. Sure, I'm easy to spot now, but one day I'll be as good as the real thing. So remember: don't trust all that you see!

● The term "deepfake" comes from joining "deep learning" and "fake"
● The first fake video system from 1997 could only change mouth movements
● Deepfake has been used to create video messages from dead people

Glossary

Android The main program on some smartphones that controls how all the other apps work.

Artificial Something that is not natural but made by people. It is often made to replace a natural object or material.

Database A set of information that is organized in such a way that it can be searched through easily.

Ethics The study of how to behave well and how to do the right things, not the wrong things.

Expert Someone who knows more about a particular subject than everyone else.

Gender Gender identity means whether you feel like a girl or a boy, or neither, or a mixture.

Hardwired A control system that is built into a system and cannot be changed. This is different from changeable controls that come from a program.

Humanoid A robot based on the body of a human.

Intelligence An ability to gather knowledge and use it to make decisions.

Interpreter Someone who translates one language into another—and maybe back again.

Laser A beam of light—or an invisible ray—that can be controlled very precisely.

Memory bank A database or another set of information stored on a computer.

Patent The right given to an inventor to be in charge of their creation so no one else can copy it without permission.

Smart Technology that uses artificial intelligence to operate without a human controller.

Source code The original code used in a program.

Strategy A plan to achieve a certain goal.

Supercomputer A stack of many small computers all working together as one.

Thought experiment A kind of puzzle that helps you understand a problem in the real world.

Translator A person or system that converts the meaning of one language into the words of another.

Ultrasound A sound that is so high-pitched that we cannot hear it.

Video platform An Internet service where people can show the videos they make and watch videos made by others.

Index

7/19/22

Main entry in **bold**